Teachers
Petit
Piaget

C. M. Charles
California State University, San Diego

Fearon Publishers, Inc.

Belmont, California

ISBN-0-8224-6780-1.

Library of Congress Catalog Card Number: 74-83219.

Printed in the United States of America.

Contents

■ PREFACE

Jean Piaget is a Swiss psychologist who has gained world fame for his research into children's thought. He has discovered some ways children think, has identified many of their mental abilities and inabilities, and has built from his observations a theory of human intellectual development.

Piaget was born in 1896. He trained first in biology, but at the age of 24 he turned his full attention to psychology. The next year, 1921, he joined the Jean Jacques Rousseau Institute in Geneva. There he has conducted most of his studies into the thought processes of children.

Piaget has reported his findings and conclusions in an astonishing number of books and articles. His ideas attracted much attention in the United States during the 1930's. Interest waned here for a time, though not in Europe, but has surged to new heights during recent years. Piaget is now considered by many to be the world's foremost theorist in human intellectual development.

Most teachers know Piaget's name, but few know much about his work, except that he believes that children move through stages of mental development, and and that they have different abilities at those different stages. In the years to come, Piaget's work will certainly attract still greater attention, for his findings abound with ideas of importance in teaching. In these pages you will find a presentation of many such ideas. They are specially selected for the insights and practical suggestions they provide teachers. Because they are greatly distilled, they cannot, of course, convey the full aura of meanings found in Piaget's original works.

But then, that is not the purpose of this book.

1
Key Ideas

We begin with a summary of Piaget's key
ideas about how children learn and grow in-
tellectually:

1. Children have mental structures that are
   different from those of adults. They are
   not adults in miniature; they have their
   own distinct ways of determining reality
   and of viewing the world.
2. Children's mental development progresses through definite stages. Those stages
   occur in a fixed sequence—a sequence
   that is the same for all children.
3. Although the stages of mental development occur in a fixed order, different
   children move from one stage to another
   at different ages. Further, a child may
   function in one stage for some matters,
   while he functions in a different stage for
   other matters.

4. Mental development is influenced by four interrelated factors:
   (a) *Maturation*—physical maturing, especially of the central nervous system.
   (b) *Experience*—handling, moving, and thinking about concrete objects, and thinking through processes involving them.
   (c) *Social Interaction*—playing, talking, and working with other people, especially other children.
   (d) *Equilibration*—the process of bringing maturation, experience, and socialization together so as to build and rebuild mental structures.

NOTE

Piaget believes that intellectual development occurs by means of two inborn attributes he calls Organization and Adaptation. Organization is the building of simpler processes—seeing, touching, naming, and so forth—into higher order mental structures. An individual thus composes his own systems for considering the world. Adaptation is the continuing change that occurs in an individual as a result of his interaction with the environment. It occurs as he assimilates experiences—fits them into his existing mental structures—and accommodates (modifies) mental structures to permit the inclusion of experiences that do not fit into existing structures.

5. For teachers, three stages of mental development are especially important:

STAGE	APPROXIMATE AVERAGE AGE AT ENTRY AND EXIT
Intuitive Thought	4–7
Concrete Operations	7–11
Formal Operations	11–15

DESCRIPTIONS

Intuitive Thought. Children reason and explain on the basis of intuitions—hunches—instead of logic. They are very poor at:
expressing the order of events
explaining relationships, especially cause-effect
understanding numbers and their relations
understanding other speakers accurately
understanding and remembering rules.

Concrete Operations. Children are developing the concepts of number, relationships, processes, and so on. They are becoming able to think through problems mentally, but they always think in terms of real (concrete) objects, not abstractions. They are developing greater ability to understand rules.

Formal Operations. Students can think using abstractions. They form theories about everything, and they are very concerned with the possible as distinct from the actual. They are reaching the level of adult thought.

6. "Operations" are actions carried out mentally. They are necessary components of rational thought. Requisite aspects of operations include:

   Conservation. The recognition that a property such as number, length, or quantity remains the same despite changes in position, shape, or grouping.

Reversibility. The recognition that any change of position, shape, order, and so on, can be reversed—that is, returned to original position, shape, or order.

7. Children's mental development imposes definite limitations on what they can learn and on how (the conditions under which) they learn.

8. Thought grows from actions, not from words.

9. Knowledge cannot be given to children. It must be discovered and constructed through the learners' activities.

10. Children learn best from concrete experiences.

11. By nature, children are continually active. They must find out about and make sense of their world. As they do so, they remake the mental structures that permit dealing with ever more complex information.

12. This remaking of mental structures makes possible genuine learning—learning that is stable and lasting. When necessary structures are not present, learning is superficial; it is not usable and it does not last.

2
Important Findings

We now turn our attention to some of Piaget's findings that seem to have special importance in the education of youth. These findings show us many things we can expect of students at various stages of intellectual development. Equally important, they show us many things we cannot expect. Included are findings related to language, rules and games, thinking and reasoning, classification and relationships, number, causality, honesty, competition, authority and obedience, guilt and punishment, and social behavior. We shall note these characteristics as they typically occur in the stages of Intuitive Thought, Concrete Operations, and Formal Operations.

AT THE STAGE OF INTUITIVE THOUGHT

6

Prior to the age of about four, the child has made huge strides in mental growth. He has become able to form "mental symbols" that stand for real objects, to use words to refer to objects and events, to make rudimentary groupings of objects (though often inconsistently), and to reason at a very simple level, probably using mental images rather than words.

At somewhere around the age of four, on the average, the child begins to move into what Piaget calls the stage of intuitive thought. We noted earlier that children at this level reason and explain on the basis of intuitions or hunches, rather than on the basis of adult-type logic. We noted, too, that in spite of the great intellectual progress they have made, they are still very poor at such things as comprehending the order of events, explaining relationships, comprehending numbers and their relationships, understanding other speakers accurately, and understanding rules.

Language

Children's verbal language at this level is of two kinds—communicative speech and egocentric speech. Communicative speech is talk intended to transmit information to others, or to ask questions of them. Egocentric speech is noncommunicative. It may consist of mimicking sounds and words, or it may be a monologue—the child merely talks as he plays, with no intention of communicating to others. It is done, seemingly, for pleasure, or perhaps because children don't yet differentiate fully between words and things or acts. Egocentric speech may comprise as much as 40 percent of the total talk of children at this stage. Nursery school and primary grade teachers should realize that it is perfectly normal. Children simply talk to themselves, even when they are in groups.

In communicative speech, children have difficulty understanding each other accurately, and they have trouble remembering more than one step, or one instruction, at a time. However, they are beginning to use words to verbalize mental images, and talk is thus a reflection of thought. They use more and more sophisticated words and expressions, which in many cases they do not understand.

Arguments

Young children argue a lot. All teachers and parents know that. Their arguments are verbal squabbles—vigorous statements of conflict. There is little interest in persuading or convincing.

Teachers should realize that arguments at this stage have powerful effects. Words and reality are not well differentiated. Name-calling does hurt feelings terribly, and it should be strongly discouraged.

Games, Rules and Competition

As the child gets older his play becomes ever more social. Previously egocentric and spontaneous, it is now increasingly related to and dependent on others. Favorite games include tag, hide and seek, searching for missing objects, and guessing games. Certain rules are becoming necessary. But they pertain to how the game is played, not to who wins or loses. (Indeed, there is still little notion of winning and losing.) Yet, a child is unlikely to know or follow more than the simplest rules. Although he is sure he knows the rules of games, he is seldom able to consider *both* his own interests and those of the group. That's why he is so likely to break the rules, though he doesn't do so maliciously.

Teachers must remember to keep rules of conduct very simple and few in number. Children will break the rules. That doesn't mean they are being ornery or defiant. They just can't remember the rules at the same time they are thinking about what they want to do.

Thinking and Reasoning

We must continually remind ourselves that children don't think like adults. At this stage they can't carry out operations in their heads—operations like adding and subtracting, following steps in problem solving, grouping and regrouping, putting events in order, naming the steps in a process, or describing how to get from one place to another. They are very poor at explaining relationships. They believe natural objects are made by men, that they exist to serve man, and that they act out of human-type motives. They are unable to think of several aspects of a situation at once. They can think of the whole, or of some of the parts, but cannot do both at the same time.

Acts are thoughts, and vice-versa. Their properties and results are seen as absolutes—right-wrong, best-worst, biggest-smallest—without variations. Children make these value judgements on the basis of first impressions, on intuitions, and on whether they afford personal pleasure or displeasure.

Classification and Relationships

During the intuitive thought stage, the child rapidly progresses from an ability to make only rudimentary groupings to an ability to classify adequately. He is becoming capable of making collections and is developing an interest in doing so. Moreover, he can make subdivisions or subgroupings within a larger group. Yet, when asked to consider both the larger group and the smaller groups within it, he is unable to do so. That is, he cannot hold in his mind simultaneously both the notion of the whole and the notion of its subparts. This inability has obvious importance for mathematics instruction, as we shall note presently.

Most youngsters at age four or five cannot arrange objects in order, such as smallest to largest, shortest to longest, and so forth. By the age of six, however, most can perform this task correctly, though they usually do so through trial and error, placing and replacing the objects on the basis of how they compare to the adjacent objects. Similarly, the child of six can usually establish one-to-one relationships between objects, but again he works on a trial-and-error basis without apparent guiding principles.

Number

Piaget has demonstrated that the child cannot adequately conceptualize number until he understands classes and relationships. Put another way, the child must be able to "conserve"—to realize that quantity remains the same regardless of how it is divided into parts—before he acquires the concept of number.

This observation takes most teachers by surprise, for they feel that as soon as a child can count he is ready to begin doing number work. Piaget's investigations show that counting and conservation of number are quite distinct operations, and that number concept does not follow on the heels of ability to count. Instead, it comes considerably later.

Primary teachers find that many children by age six or even earlier can learn some basic number facts in addition and subtraction. Piaget notes this ability, too, but maintains that children can do number operations with understanding only when they have become able to establish one-to-one correspondence between objects in sets and conserve that correspondence—that is, realize the number doesn't change when the objects are rearranged. Some of Piaget's ideas about the development of number concept are further explained in Appendix B.

Honesty

Studies have shown that teachers consider dishonesty a very serious character flaw. They feel that lying, for example, indicates a depraved state, and that it must never be tolerated.

Piaget reminds us that "lying" is common to virtually all children at the intuitive stage. Perhaps lying is not the word to use, for seldom does the child intend to deceive. The facts get mixed up in his mind—he still may not altogether differentiate fact from fiction; the story may just sound better that way; or if one child relates an experience, others will claim to have done the same.

Competition

Competition in games and work means virtually nothing to the child at this stage. He has little idea of the meaning of winning, losing, or outdoing others. Each child plays or works for himself and for the fun of the activity. He does not play against others.

Authority and Obedience

At ages four and five, most children are very obedient to adults. Adult ways are fair ways. To be good is to be obedient; to be bad is to be disobedient. This is an individual matter; children do not comprehend group responsibility. Thus they do not expect the entire group to be punished for the misbehaviors of a few. Moreover, there is nothing wrong with disobedience in itself— it is not wrong. It is simply a violation of adult authority, and as such it is quite acceptable that it should bring punishment. The misbehaving child seldom feels guilt for his actions, yet adult reproof for misbehavior is expected. Misdeeds by other children always call for adult punishment.

By the age of six or seven, however, this total acceptance of adult authority begins to waver. Children note inconsistencies in the ways adults behave. Despite this, most children are still quite willing to accept the authority of adults.

Guilt and Punishment

As noted, guilt is nothing more than getting caught misbehaving, and misbehavior is merely disobedience to adult rules. There is nothing wrong with misbehavior as such. Yet, punishment is the natural consequence of misbehavior, and it is to be expected. It is just. It is necessary.

Social Behavior

We saw earlier that much of the child's talk at the beginning of this stage is egocentric. As he grows to ages six and seven, his social interests increase. He engages in more communicative and less egocentric talk, although the latter type appears and reappears for several years. Games, too, are becoming increasingly social. Other participants are required, not simply tolerated. Children at this stage are becoming highly imitative of each other. If one makes a funny noise or gesture, a number of others will repeat it.

AT THE STAGE OF CONCRETE OPERATIONS

On the average, the child at about seven years of age begins to move from the stage of intuitive thought into the stage of concrete operations. Note again that age seven is an average age. Some children begin the transition earlier; others begin it later. And no child makes the transition as a clean break. A given child may, for example, begin thinking at the concrete operations stage with regard to the conservation of number. But he may still function in the intuitive thought stage with regard to the conservation of volume. In general, we can say that the transition occurs first for what we would consider simpler operations, such as the conservation of length, and later for more complex operations, such as the conservation of volume. For further clarification of the nature of these operations, refer to Appendix B.

Capacities for performing concrete operations develop one by one, rather than all at once. We must realize that these new understandings are occurring at the expense of former beliefs that are not all that easily shaken off. We can expect that the transitional child, when under stress, will tend to revert to earlier ideas and behaviors.

But what, then, are some of the essential differences between children's abilities in the two stages—intuitive thought as compared to concrete operations? The main difference is that the child becomes able to carry out operations mentally, or "in his head." That is, he can put ideas in sequence, remember the whole while dividing it into parts, and reverse these acts to return the parts to their original states. In more technical terms, the child can conserve, and he can reverse operations. "Conserve" refers to the ability to consider, at the same time, both the whole and various arrangements of its parts. The child sees that the whole and its parts are reciprocal, and he sees how they fit together. He also sees how a quantity remains the same despite distortions: For example, he becomes aware that there is still the same amount of clay when a lump is rolled into a "rope."

"Reverse" refers to the ability to stop processes at any point and return them, at least mentally, to their original state. If you separate ten marbles into groups of five, you can reverse the process by recombining the two groups of five into a single group of ten. The significance of this ability can hardly be over-emphasized. The child can now, for the first time, explore several different routes in the solution of a problem. When one of them doesn't work out, he can return to the beginning and start over again. That is, he can test his hunches mentally, always able to go back and start over again if necessary.

In summary, the child is said to be functioning at the stage of concrete operations when he can organize experience into a consistent whole, can make rational sense of his experiences, can make classifications and arrangements, can conserve those classifications and arrangements, can reverse operations he performs on them, and can conceive of an event from different perspectives simultaneously.

In the first part of this chapter we noted several specific characteristics of children at the intuitive thought stage. Now let's see how children change with regard to some of those same characteristics when they move into the stage of concrete operations.

Language

Previously, much of the child's talk was egocentric, or noncommunicative. Now it has become much more communicative, though he will still be observed talking to himself occasionally. Words have also become the tool of the thinking process—the child increasingly thinks with words rather than visualizations. But the words must always relate back to concrete experiences. The child cannot yet deal with pure abstractions. At this stage he uses many words of high degrees of sophistication, though he is often only vaguely aware of their meanings.

Arguments

The child is still highly argumentative, especially with other children though not so much with adults, whose authority he seldom challenges directly. Arguments tend to be loud and abusive. Words still hurt sorely. But there is a growing note of reason and persuasion.

Games, Rules, and Competition

Play is becoming much more collective and less individualistic. Cooperation and group effort are required. By around age nine, on the average, children show a desire for definite rules to regulate play. While any individual child may be quite willing to fudge a bit on following the rules, he will be thoroughly unwilling for another child to do so. He decries rule violations, and a great percentage of arguments among children come from disputes about whether the rules of a game have been properly followed.

Along with the growing necessity for rules comes a strongly emerging sense of competition. Children are still quite cooperative in most group endeavors, and they will continue so. But when it comes to games, winning has become very important. At the same time, losing becomes almost intolerable for many children. Losing may produce temper tantrums, aggression, and crying. This does not mean that children cannot tolerate being something other than first in most of their activities. But in sports and games, they need help in learning to lose gracefully.

Thinking and Reasoning

Several characteristics of thinking and reasoning were mentioned in the introductory paragraphs of this section, which described the transition of children to the stage of concrete operations. Basically, we noted that the child has become much more adult-like in his thought processes. He can perform operations mentally, though he continues to think of real objects as he does so. He can conserve quantity, length, number, etc.—that is, hold it constant in his mind despite regrouping of parts or changes in appearance. He can reverse operations—undo them, mentally, thus permitting mental exploration of various procedures with the ability to return to the beginning whenever necessary to begin anew. Increasingly, he has become able to use words and other symbols to stand for concrete objects as he carries out his mental explorations.

Classification and Relationships

The child's newly acquired abilities allow him to do numbers of things he couldn't do before, especially in the sciences and mathematics. Performing experiments and making logical explanations and predictions are examples. He is becoming increasingly able to make valid relationships among the things he observes. In fact, extensive opportunity for observation and manipulation of objects seems highly important for mental growth. The explanations he makes for what he observes slowly change from the earlier concentration on artificialism and animism to more "natural" explanations. For a detailed description of the kinds of explanations children make about natural phenomena, refer to Appendix A.

Number and Mathematics

As we already noted, the child has developed the mental capacity to deal effectively with number and number operations. He can now make accurate one-to-one relationships. He can conserve number, and show this conservation through grouping and regrouping accurately. He can also measure properly, because he has become able to conserve length and has, or will soon have, become able to conserve mass. This ability permits the use of rulers, scales, and other measuring devices.

Because the mental operations the child performs are still based on his visualization of real, concrete objects, activities in mathematics must still place heavy emphasis on the manipulation of objects.

Honesty

Earlier, the child "lied" as a matter of course—he simply embellished, fabricated, or repeated the experiences of others without any real intent to deceive. Now, the child has a growing concept of honesty. He has become able to disassociate "truth" from temporary and specific situations (that is, he sees truth as an idea, instead of merely a part of a specific situation). He may, if conditions warrant, make conscious attempts to deceive through lying. He has a concept of morality. He sees that the more a lie intends to deceive, the worse it is. All in all, he has developed a conscience—one that is based at least in part on respect for others and on an awareness for collective obedience to rules and expectations.

Authority and Obedience

The child is still quite obedient to adults and recognizes their authority. However, he has begun to lose his belief that they are always totally right. He has by now become aware of too many inconsistencies, too many adult errors. At the same time, he has a growing awareness of the ways rules are made. He develops, too, a reliance on peer norms for guidance. He will most often obey adults, even when they make unreasonable demands. But he may talk back, inside himself, and he will begin to heap verbal abuse on absent adult authorities when talking with his friends.

Guilt and Punishment

Since the child has begun developing a conscience, he has a growing sense of right and wrong. He will know it when he does wrong things, whether or not he is being directly disobedient to an adult.

Seldom does any child select punishment as the due consequence of his own wrongdoing. Yet, he still sees punishment as the proper consequence of the wrongdoing of others. He does insist, however, on complete impartiality from adults in the enforcement of rules and the taking of disciplinary actions. To be fair, the punishment should exactly compensate for the wrong that has been done. He sees inconsistent punishment as very unfair. He strongly resents group punishment for the guilt of a few.

Social Behavior

One of the most notable characteristics of children at this stage is the decrease in the size of their families. Pets lose their special status as immediate members of the family—the equivalent of brothers and sisters. However, that doesn't mean they become less valued. To judge from the quantity of sibling quarreling, pets may even move up a notch in the hierarchy.

Otherwise, children are growing in the respect they hold for each other. There is an increasing desire to be with other children, to have group names, and to begin to form gangs, clubs, and cliques.

And, yes, at this stage children are coming to see each other in a new light—the light of social position.

AT THE STAGE OF FORMAL OPERATIONS

Toward the end of the elementary grades, at an average age of about eleven, children begin moving out of the concrete operations stage and into the stage of formal operations. This is again a very significant point in the course of intellectual development. Here the child is moving into adult-type thought. That doesn't mean he can make decisions as well as an adult, or solve problems as well, or be as poised in new situations. It is just that his thought processes are similar to those of the adult. He is becoming able to think about abstract ideas, and to carry out operations using abstractions that have no concrete, tangible referents. This ability to deal with abstractions gives the individual powerful new tools for structuring his world. He can think beyond the real world and beyond the present. He no longer has to limit himself to symbols that stand for real things (although most of us do so most of the time). He can make effective use of such concepts as love, hate, honesty, and loyalty; of negative numbers, forces, speeds, time, and atomic particles. To put it another way, he can think about thought. At an average age of about fifteen, the individual has reached intellectual maturity. His mental workings have reached their highest level of development. They will not become more sophisticated or complex. Of course they may, through practice, become more efficient, more consistent. The individual will later become much wiser. But nonetheless, for the first time, really, he thinks in the same way that adults think. For the first time, teachers can expect their students' perceptions to resemble their own.

Language

Once the student becomes able to use abstractions, he becomes even more influenced by formal language. He sees that language gives him a system of concepts, ideas, classifications, and relationships, that are conventional—conventional in the sense that they reflect meanings agreed upon by people in general. More than ever he uses language as the vehicle of thought, especially for abstract thought where concrete objects do not exist.

Thinking and Reasoning

Our student has become a full-blown theoretician. If not accurate, he is at least prolific. He composes theories about everything. Everything has an explanation, a place. Prescriptive theories of right and wrong abound.

This tendency to form hypotheses and theories hinges on a newly acquired ability to do propositional thinking—the "if . . . then" kind of thinking. There is no need to proceed from the actual to the theoretical, as, for example, "All cats are good climbers and jumpers. They are good climbers and jumpers because . . ." Instead, one can as easily begin with the theory and move back to particulars, as in, for instance, "Good jumping and climbing ability are helpful in survival. That's probably why many different animals, such as the cat, can jump and climb so well."

In other words, reasoning now treats the possible fully as much as it does the actual. Reality is still important, but no more so than possibility. The exercise of this new power to deal with the "right" and the "possible" in abstract terms produces the idealism that is characteristic of adolescence and postadolescence. Again, the earlier-acquired ability to reverse operations permits the mental exploration of hypotheses. You can test them out of your mind. If they don't work out well, you can return to the beginning and take a new tack.

Science and Math

It is not until this stage of mental development that an adequate notion of experimentation emerges. The student can think "If I do thus and thus, so and so will result." Then he can set up an experiment to find out if he is right. He is just now beginning to understand a number of geometric relationships, questions dealing with proportion, the general notion of relativity, and the link between actions and reactions. At the same time his sense of awe about nature balloons. He experiences feelings of inadequacy. He has rejected animism, but the idea of physical forces in equilibrium (accounting for the movements and positions of objects in the world) astounds him.

Morality and Punishment

A lie is now seen as anything intentionally false. Rules and laws must be morally right and fairly applied. Breaking the rules is no longer seen as absolutely wrong. Punishment for breaking the rules, for instance, must take into account factors such as intent to break the rule, age of the violator, and his previous record of behavior. Many rules may be seen as "wrong"; therefore, no harm is done in breaking them. Wrongdoing still deserves punishment, but only for the wrongdoer. Group punishment, when there are innocent menbers of the group, is viewed as gross injustice.

Social Behavior

One of the major interests is now the consideration of various social points of view. The student likes to weigh them, clarify them, and evaluate them, one against the other. He thinks of politics, institutions, human relations, and so forth. His theorizing about ideal systems may lead him to be overly critical and rejecting of faults he sees in actuality. Yet, seldom will he seriously commit himself to any new social idea. He may scathingly reject, in language, existing social arrangements and values. Yet, his actions usually reflect an adherence to the prevailing arrangements and values.

3
Implications for Teaching

Piaget's main concern has not been with problems of teaching. Yet even the most casual reader has to be struck by the power of his ideas when they are applied to instructing the young. This chapter will pull many of those ideas together within areas that concern every teacher.

Abilities of Children

At times children surprise us with what they can do. At other times they surprise us with what they cannot do. Many children make unexpectedly rapid advances in verbal ability. Vocabulary grows with astounding speed. We hear young children use words typical of adult speech, and we look on them as very precocious.

But this verbal ability of children often causes us to make false assessments of their abilities. The ability to use big words (although usually without comprehension of what they mean) does not always mean that children have developed mental structures that allow them to use logic, to relate cause and effect adequately, to conserve quantity, or to reverse processes, all of which are requisites for comprehension in science experimentation and number operations. Moreover, sets of rules and lists of steps in directions may be beyond the grasp of these children.

Piaget's work tells us much about what to expect of children at different stages of their development. It also tells us how to identify the stage or stages at which a given child is functioning in different task areas. By paying attention to his findings, teachers can proceed on a realistic basis, providing practice and help that are within children's capabilities, while avoiding attempts to instruct in matters beyond the child's functional capabilities—an undertaking that brings only frustration to both student and teacher.

Activities

Children must act. Seldom are they inactive for more than a few minutes during their waking hours. To force them to be still and quiet in school goes strongly against their natures, and is bound to result in a struggle between teachers' wills and students' needs.

Teachers do better to capitalize on the native traits of children. They can do this by providing a wealth of materials for children to look at, touch, handle, and move about. Such materials should be used to a far greater degree than is now common in schools. Verbal interaction among students should be allowed and encouraged. Group activities that involve cooperation and discussion should comprise a significant part of the school day.

Classroom

The classroom should be arranged and equipped to enhance an activity-oriented curriculum. Quantities of materials should be provided in convenient work areas in the room. (Noisier activities should be held at one end of the room, and quieter activities at the other.) Some spaces should be set aside for individual activities, others for small group activities. Room dividers, if used, should be easily movable so the entire class has sufficient space to meet together for large group activities.

Climate

The psychological climate within the classroom is determined primarily by the teacher. Piaget's conclusions suggest that this climate should be free and spontaneous. This should not be interpreted as a *laissez-faire* climate, where the teacher provides neither direction nor help. Rather, the teacher provides materials, suggests activities, works alongside, and helps students. Spontaneous talk is allowed, and the sharing of ideas is encouraged. The teacher sees to it that active, productive work activities are maximized, and that chaos does not occur.

Facilitation

The teacher's main job is not to transmit knowledge. Rather, it is to ensure that children act, physically and mentally. Those acts should be of types that play roles in human development, especially social interactions that stress language and the manipulation of objects to solve problems.

This job requires that teachers comprehend the abilities of children and how they learn best. They must improve their skills in watching and listening to children at work so they can give the right kind of help when it is needed. They must be wary of the common assumptions that children learn like adults do and that they learn best through reading and listening in always quiet surroundings.

Individualization

To be consistent with Piaget's ideas, individualization should be thought of as attempting to do what is best for each child—what will do most to further his development. At times this will be individual activity, at times group activity. Sometimes the activities will be selected by individuals, at other times the teacher or the group will select them.

Even though many teachers are hesitant to allow students to select their own activities for the day, there is reason to believe that if children are provided adequate materials and options, they will select activities that will be consistent with the functional level (stage) of their intellectual development. Teachers can vary the activity options available to individual students each day to be sure they have an adequate variety of experiences.

Planning

Children take a more active role in their schooling when they are brought into the processes of planning and selecting their learning activities. Guidance is always provided by the teacher, who interprets general goals and curriculum guidelines. Students choose among options suggested by the teacher, and sometimes suggest options of their own. They participate in planning for group activities of various kinds. When given the opportunity, children will usually make reasonable decisions about the activities in which they are to engage.

Rules of Conduct

Young children can remember a few simple rules of conduct, yet paradoxically they are almost certain to break them often. They will usually obey rules to please the teacher and because of their bending to adult authority, not because they recognize the necessity for rules to affect them personally. When rules conflict with their own desires, they will break them, though not maliciously. Breaking rules brings no remorse, no feelings of guilt. Still, some punishment is seen as the just consequence of breaking adults rules.

Socialization

Piaget stresses social interaction as a necessary condition for intellectual development. Many people believe that Piaget's theory stresses only the maturation of the nervous system and experience with concrete objects. However, these components, essential as they are, are not enough. Children need to talk, discuss, and dispute with other children. Teachers must see that social interaction, stressing language, is given a prominent place in the daily instructional program. This can be accomplished through inclusion of such activities as group projects, group discussions, group problem solving, role playing, dramatic play, and class debates.

Work

We read and hear much about children's short attention spans, about how they can pay attention to a given task for only a few minutes at a stretch. It would be more proper to refer to those periods as forced attention spans. It is true that children can force their attentions for very short lengths of time, when the tasks are not interesting. The same thing, after all, is true for adults. But children will pay attention and work long at tasks that involve objects to manipulate, bodily movement, and talk. Similarly, they will avidly watch and listen to presentations, such as stories, plays, and animated cartoons, that incorporate many different sounds, movements, and colors.

In short, children will work hard at what adults call play. They don't make the distinction between the two at first; some things are worth doing, others simply aren't. Later they do make a distinction that is rather unfortunate—play is what's fun; work is what's dull.

Appendix

A / CHILDREN'S IDEAS ABOUT CAUSES

Have you ever asked young children about the things around them—things like the moon and wind, waves and shadows? Where they came from and what makes them move? Their answers will surprise you. And they will inform you, too, about the way children see the world and explain it, and about the progressive stages in their ability to explain causes.

Children keep busy asking questions. They want to know the "why" of everything. After a while, this questioning irritates adults, and we find ways of cutting off the questions. Yet, we could learn a great deal about the children we teach if we would turn things around and begin asking them questions. Not on tests, where they learn to be worried and nervous about getting the "right answer." But just informally, offhand. Questions about how a bicycle or a jet plane works. About why dogs can run so fast. Or why the sun seems to follow us when we walk.

Piaget used that type of question—the kind of question that calls forth an explanation—in some of his studies on the way children think. In particular, he gave attention to the explanations they make about machines, natural phenomena, their origins, and their movements. For Piaget, those studies revealed some consistent patterns of development through which children progress in their thinking. They help teachers by showing kinds of explanations children make at different age levels. Those explanations tell us something about what goes on in the children's minds.

The cause-effect relationship is extremely important in all our lives. It is basic to the sciences and it permits us to explain, predict, and control numbers of phenomena in our environment.

Piaget recognized that most of us know very little indeed about the growth of conceptions of causality. Does the cause-effect concept emerge, full grown, along with language? Or does it develop somewhat apart from the ability to speak? Does ability to explain follow the same pattern regardless of the topic? What can we expect a child's ideas of causality to be when he enters school, and as he progresses through school?

In analyzing children's answers to questions, Piaget identified three main processes and three main periods in the development of children's explanations of causality.

Major Processes

Piaget saw the whole of the development of children's explanations of causality reflected in three great processes occurring *simultaneously*. He described those processes as "progressive change"

- from realism to objectivity
- from realism to reciprocity
- from realism to relativity.

From Realism to Objectivity

The child at age three puts the whole content of his consciousness on the same plane. He does not distinguish between the "I" on one hand and the people and things of the external world on the other. "Realism" is the name Piaget used to refer to this early failure to distinguish clearly between the "self" and "all else."

Piaget used the term "objectivity" to refer to a child's differentiation between his "self" and the rest of the world. Slowly he becomes conscious of the "I," and so is able to distinguish, very roughly at first, between external fact and internal interpretation.

It must be emphasized that this objectivity—this differentiation between external fact and internal interpretation—develops slowly. The initial realism is very persistent. It erodes by slow degrees, and in truth it never completely disappears. We continue throughout life incapable of fully removing the effects of our biases and prejudices on our perception of the world.

Piaget noted how slowly this evolution occurs, and he remarked on "adherences" that remain as children progress through stages of mental development. Adherences are fragments of internal experience that children superimpose over external experiences. Chief among them are *animism* and *artificialism*.

In the *animism* adherence, inanimate things such as wind, trees, sun, automobiles, and so forth, are thought to have life, feelings, intentions, and even the ability to move on their own. They seem to participate actively in one's life.

The *artificialism* adherence suggests that things in the external world are made for people. Everything about them is willed and intentional. They exist for people, and most of them work toward good. Young children, when asked about why there are such things as a sun, moon, or sky, often reply that they exist to give us light, wind, and so forth.

From Realism to Reciprocity

Reciprocity refers to a condition where the child has come to realize that other people have opinions and points of view separate from his own. For example, some children as late as the age of eight still see no difficulty with their perception that the sun and moon follow them about as they walk. By the age of nine, however, most are beginning to realize that the sun is really just very high, and it seems to *everybody* that it follows along. They are coming slowly to believe that one's ideas and beliefs are not absolute, that other people have similar ones, and that reality does not reside solely in one person's thoughts. Other ideas of other people grow in importance.

From Realism to Relativity

As children first develop consciousness of objects and movements, they see all values as absolute. A pebble is light, a brick is heavy. A snail is slow, a bicycle is fast. Sunlight is bright, shadow is dim. As children mature, however, they begin to see values as relative. A pebble is heavy for an ant, a brick is light for an elephant. Compared to a bicycle, a turtle is slow, but compared to an inchworm it is fast.

Major Periods

The three major processes we examined occur simultaneously and gradually through three distinct phases, or periods.

The First Period

The first period occupies roughly the years three through five. This is a period in which children seek reasons for everything. They constantly ask the question "why?". If we turn the question back to them—ask them to tell us why something is the way it is, how it came to be, what it is for—they will make explanations of types that Piaget called motivational, phenomenistic, finalistic, magical, and moralistic.

Motivational explanations offer human-type motivation as the cause of everything. Nightmares are sent to us because we have been bad; summer showers fall because someone, or something, wants us to be cooler. Piaget found this type of thinking very long-lived. Anthropologists find it predominant in many prescientific societies of the present day.

Phenomenistic explanations relate two facts that occur close together in time or space. Often, one may be seen as causing the other. The moon stays up in the sky for astronauts to land on; it's also there to make light.

Finalistic explanations show that things are so because they are, and no further thought is given. Fish have fins because they are part of fish; the river runs because it runs to the sea.

Magical explanations hold that one's gestures, thoughts, and words influence people and events. To say harmful words is to harm someone.

Moralistic explanations show that events occur because they have to; it would not be right if they didn't. Thus, boats float so they won't sink, and the sun must set so we can have night.

The Second Period

The second period in the development of children's explanations of causality occupies roughly the ages five through eight. Children continue to seek reasons avidly, though the number of "why" questions begins to diminish. Piaget found that the explanations they provide when questioned are predominantly of the types he called artificialist and animistic.

Artificialist explanations reveal the belief that objects and occurrences are man-made. When asked about the origin of the sun, for example, children will often answer that some men made it. Why? So we can have light.

Animistic explanations show nonliving things behaving as if they had life and consciousness. Rocks grow biologically, there on the ground. Clouds move so they can get to different places. Lightening flashes to make loud noise or to scare us.

The Third Period

The third period in the development of children's explanations of causality occupies roughly the ages eight to eleven. In this period there is a gradual supplanting of previous types of explanation by those Piaget called mechanistic, generative, and logical. By the end of this period the typical child will have reached a level where he can think in abstract terms and make logical explanations. Moreover, he sees causal relationships as reversible—water frozen into ice can be restored to water; a stone crushed to bits can, theoretically, be reassembled into its original form. The abilities to abstract, reverse, and use logic give the child of 11 to 12 the capability for adult-type thought.

Mechanistic explanations emerge as animism disappears. Now a bicycle goes because of its pedals; clouds move because of the wind; cars go because of their steering wheels, and electric lights burn because you plug them in.

Generative explanations refer to origins of things rather than to their movements. Earlier, the child thought that natural objects in his surroundings were made by men. Now he thinks of them as generated by other objects. The sun originated from a cloud; clouds come from smoke, etc.

Logical explanations begin to grow in most children at around age 10 to 11, and they play an increasingly important role in thought. Logic depends on "sufficient reason"—ample evidence considered in an open-minded way. It includes both induction (generalizations made from observations) and deduction (conclusions derived through syllogistic reasoning).

Questions and Questioning

Many allusions have been made in these pages to questions Piaget asks children. The following samples are included to give you a clearer conception of his style of questioning and of the types of questions he uses. The following excerpt is taken from Piaget's *The Child's Conception of Physical Causality* (The Humanities Press, Inc., 1951). The subsequent sample questions and answers are adapted from the same source.

QUESTIONING A FIVE-YEAR-OLD CHILD ABOUT SHADOWS

You know what a shadow is?
Yes, it's the trees that make them, under the tree.
Why is there a shadow under the tree?
Because there are a lot of leaves. The leaves make it.

How do they do it?
Because they are pink.
What does that do?
It makes a shadow.
Why?
Because inside the leaves it is night inside.
Why?
Because it's day on top.
Etc.

In the following sample questions and answers, you must remember one thing: These responses cannot be considered "typical" of the age indicated, because there is a sizable variation from one child to another as regards the age at which certain kinds of explanations are made.

QUESTION TOPIC	SAMPLE EXPLANATIONS BY AGES	TYPE OF EXPLANATION*
Centrifugal Force		
(A penny is swung overhead in an open container attached to strings.) *Why doesn't the penny fall out?*	(6) The sides hold it back.	Phenomenistic
	(8) It's going around fast.	Phenomenistic
	(10) The air holds it in.	Mechanistic
Origin of Wind		
Where does the wind come from?	(6) Men blew it.	Artificialist
	(8) From the sky, clouds.	Generative
	(9) Tree branches make it.	Generative

*Not identified as such by Piaget. Solely the writer's interpretation.

QUESTION TOPIC	SAMPLE EXPLANATIONS BY AGES	TYPE OF EXPLANATION
Movement of Clouds		
What makes clouds move?	(5) You can make clouds move.	Artificialist
	(6) They follow us.	Animistic
	(7) They move along by themselves.	Animistic
	(8) The air pushes them.	Mechanistic
Movement of Sun and Moon		
If you go for a walk in the evening, does the moon stay still?	(4) No, it follows me.	Animistic
Why does the sun move along?	(6) To keep us warm.	Motivational
How does the sun move along?	(7) The clouds move it.	Mechanistic
	(8) All by itself.	Animistic
Water Movements		
What are waves? What makes them?	(6) A man.	Artificialist
	(7) The water moves, pushes.	Animistic
	(10) It's the air. The wind.	Logical
Why does the water in the river move along?	(5) The boats.	Phenomenistic
	(8) Stones in the river make a current.	Phenomenistic

QUESTION TOPIC	SAMPLE EXPLANATIONS BY AGES	TYPE OF EXPLANATION
	(9) Other water coming behind pushes it.	Mechanistic
	(11) It's heavy. It goes down hill like falling.	Logical

Objects That Don't Fall

QUESTION TOPIC	SAMPLE EXPLANATIONS BY AGES	TYPE OF EXPLANATION
Why don't the clouds fall down?	(5) God holds them.	Magical
	(7) The sky holds them.	Phenomenistic
	(9) The air lifts them.	Mechanistic
	(10) They can't. They are light.	Logical
How does the sun stay up there?	(6) Because it wants to give light.	Motivational
	(8) The sky and clouds hold it.	Phenomenistic

Things That Float

QUESTION TOPIC	SAMPLE EXPLANATIONS BY AGES	TYPE OF EXPLANATION
Why does a heavy boat float on top of the water?	(4) Boats stay on top of the water.	Finalistic
	(10) The water is heavier than wood.	Logical

Displacement in Liquids

QUESTION TOPIC	SAMPLE EXPLANATIONS BY AGES	TYPE OF EXPLANATION
Show the child a pebble and a glass ¾ filled with water. *I'm going to put this*	(7) Will stay the same. (*Why?*) It has to stay the same.	Moralistic

QUESTION TOPIC	SAMPLE EXPLANATIONS BY AGES		TYPE OF EXPLANATION
pebble into the water. Will the water go up, or down, or stay the same?	(8)	Will go down. (*Why?*) Cause the pebble is heavy.	Mechanistic
	(11)	Rise. (*Why?*) The pebble takes up space.	Logical
Shadows			
Cast the shadow of your hand on a table. *Why is there a shadow here?*	(6)	Because there is a hand.	Finalistic
	(8)	It comes from the hand.	Generative
	(10)	The light comes from there. It's a place where there's no light.	Logical
Machines			
What makes a bicycle go?	(4)	The wheels.	Phenomenistic
	(6)	You pedal with your feet.	Mechanistic
	(10)	When you pedal there's a chain that makes the wheels go round.	Logical
How does a car go?	(6)	You put gas in it.	Phenomenistic
	(9)	The engine. It goes to the wheels.	Mechanistic

Appendix

B / MENTAL READINESS FOR MATHEMATICS

Imagine a child who has learned to count. Not merely to count to ten by rote, but to count actual objects, correctly, to twenty and beyond. Is this child now ready to add and subtract, and soon to multiply and divide? Does he have the mental structures—the capabilities—to perform these fundamental operations of quantity and number? Appearances, common sense, and intuition all seem to answer yes, he is ready.

Piaget, however, has found that the opposite is often true, that the child may still be some time away from developing the mental requisites for performing these operations. Contrary to appearances, the ability to add and subtract does not follow directly on the heels of the ability to count. Rather, it comes later, *only when the child conceptu-*

alizes number as constant and composed of elements that can be grouped and regrouped in various ways. This means he must grasp the idea that number represents units, that the units can be put in one-to-one relationships and that the units can be put into sequence.

How can we know when a child has developed such a concept of number? We can't expect him to answer that question for us, at least not directly. His chronological age gives us only vague guidance: Children reach the required levels at different ages, and they develop certain of the abilities (such as one-to-one correspondence) before they develop others (such as conservation of correspondence).

Perhaps the best means for answering the question is seen in the sorts of tasks Piaget used when he investigated children's concepts of number. The following pages contain informal tests patterned after some of Piaget's. Until a child can perform most of them correctly, it is questionable that he is ready for the customary beginning instruction in addition and subtraction.

As you use these tests, doubts will rise in your mind. Most children won't be able to perform them correctly until somewhere around the age of seven, and some will be as old as eight or more. Yet, your experience may have shown you many six-year-olds, and even some five-year-olds, who could tell you that "2 + 2 = 4, 2 + 4 = 6" and so on. Piaget stresses that while young children can be taught to repeat "2 + 4 = 6", there is no true assimilation of such a concept until the child is capable of seeing that 6 is a totality, containing 2 and 4 as parts, and he is capable of grouping various combinations to make 6.

Few teachers will dispute the desirability of true assimilation—what we might think of as understanding with ability to apply knowledge and skill. Yet we customarily try to teach number operations to first and second grade children, many of whom, try as they (and we) might, cannot adequately conceptualize these operations.

The tests that follow can help answer the question of whether a given child is ready to profit, with "true assimilation," from basic instruction in the processes of addition and subtraction.

TEST I. CONSERVATION OF QUANTITY

Materials Needed
    Four identical transparent plastic glasses
    One transparent glass, taller and thinner than the others
    Red liquid (water with food coloring)
    Green liquid

Directions

1. Fill one of the plastic glasses 3/4 full with red liquid, place it before the child and say "Here's one for you, but it's not to drink."

2. Fill another plastic glass to exactly the same level with green liquid and say "And here's one for me. Do I have the same amount as you?" (Be sure that the child sees they are the same.)
3. Pour your glass of green liquid into two other plastic glasses, and ask "Do we now have the same? If mine were lemonade and yours were orangeade, would we have the same amount to drink?"

NOTE

Ask clarifying questions as necessary. If the child answers, "yes," ask, "How do you know?" If the child answers "No, they aren't the same now," ask "But weren't they the same before? What has changed? Don't they still make the same as before? Are they really different or do they just look that way?"

4. Pour your two glasses of green liquid together into the tall thin glass. Ask "Who has more now?" Ask clarifying questions as necessary.
5. If the child has seen the red and green liquid as unequal quantities, ask "What must we do to make them the same again?"
6. Pour the green liquid back into the original glass. Ask "Are they the same now?"

Discussion

Young children below the *average* age of about seven (please remember that different children acquire the necessary abilities at different age levels) do not believe that the quantity of liquid stays the same when the shape or number of containers changes. They believe the quantity changes with the shape of the container. The explanation for this is that apparently the child can reason with respect to only one dimension at a time (height or width); he cannot coordinate two or more dimensions in his thinking.

Later, he becomes sure the quantities are the same under the various conditions. He can coordinate two or more dimensions, so as to see that, for example, increase in height is compensated by decrease in width.

This idea of permanence of quantity, even when changed in shape or broken into parts, is essential to the understanding of number.

TEST II. CORRESPONDENCE OF QUANTITY

One way to compare quantities is to compare dimensions. That was done in Test I. Another way to compare quantities is to make one-to-one correspondence between elements of quantities (sets), as shown in Test II.

Materials Needed

Six plastic glasses
Eighteen toothpicks

Directions

1. Place the six glasses before the child. Say, "We need a toothpick for each glass. Take just the same number of toothpicks as there are glasses—one toothpick for each glass."
2. When the child has finished, ask, "Are there as many toothpicks as glasses? Show me."

   NOTE

   Some children will be unable to complete this task correctly. For them the test ends here.

3. For children who perform the first two steps correctly, check to see whether they still

think the sets are equal when the position of

the glasses and toothpicks is changed, like
this:

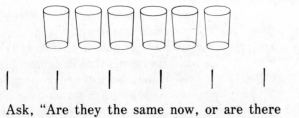

Ask, "Are they the same now, or are there
more glasses or more toothpicks?" Follow with
clarifying questions as necessary; for example,
"Count them again; are they the same? Where
are there more? How can we make them the
same?"

4. Rearrange the glasses and toothpicks like this:

Ask the same questions as in Step 3.
5. If the child is successful, see whether he can
   make a two-to-one correspondence—two
   toothpicks for each glass.

Discussion

The child does not have the necessary notions for
learning number operations unless he sees permanence and equivalence of sets irrespective of the
distribution of elements.

TEST III. CORRESPONDENCE OF SET ELEMENTS IN SERIES

A series is a group of things standing in some kind of order—an ordered arrangement. Piaget advises that "all correspondence presupposes seriation, and when seriation is not possible, neither is serial correspondence." He means that if elements of sets cannot be placed in some sort of order—smallest to largest, lightest to darkest, and so on—they cannot be put into one-to-one correspondence with elements of another set that are in serial order. Test III determines whether a child can put objects into series, whether he can make one-to-one correspondence between two series, and whether he can maintain the correspondence even when set elements are rearranged.

Materials Needed

Obtain a 3-foot length of ½ inch square wooden stick. Cut ten lengths from it, so that the shortest is 2¼", the next 2½", the next 2¾", and so on.

Also obtain a 2-foot length of stick that is smaller in diameter than the one mentioned above. Cut ten lengths from it. Make the shortest 1", the next 1¼", the next 1½", and so on.

Directions

1. Place the lengths of wood of the larger diameter on the table in front of the child and say, "These are boys (or girls). We want them to lie down for their naps, in a line with the shortest boy on one end and the tallest on the other end. Make them lie so that each boy is just a little bit taller (or shorter) than the one lying next to him."

   Ask clarifying questions as necessary. If the child cannot make the indicated arrangement, the test ends. If he can make the arrangement,

proceed with the following step.

2. Place the lengths of wood with the smaller diameter near the "boys." Say, "These are baseball bats, all of different sizes. Each boy should have the bat that belongs to him. We want the smallest boy to have the shortest bat and the largest boy to have the longest bat." If the child can make the arrangement, proceed to the next step.

3. Rearrange the boys and bats by putting the boys closer together and the bats farther apart, like this:

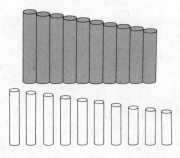

Touch one of the boys and ask "Which bat will this one take?" Continue the procedure with four or five of the other boys.

4. Reverse the order of either the boys or the bats, like this:

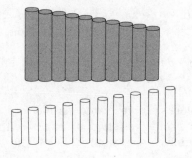

Ask "Which bat will this boy take? Why? How do you know?"

5. Disarrange either the boys or the bats, so they are no longer in order. Point to a boy and ask, "Which bat will this boy take?" The child may make many errors here, so follow up with such comments as "How do you know? Show me."

TEST IV. FUNDAMENTALS OF ADDITION

This test is used to determine whether children can conceptualize that partial classes are included in wider classes.

Materials Needed

Twenty wooden cubes—eighteen red and two yellow. (Pieces of colored breakfast cereal, such as Trix, can serve as well. If cereal is used, change the wording appropriately in the directions that follow.)

A strip of paper with twenty squares drawn in a row (or circles, if you use cereal), the first eighteen in red and the last two in yellow. You can make a quantity of these papers by preparing a Ditto master using red and yellow carbon.)

Directions

1. Show the blocks to the child. Arrange them in a row, with the two yellow ones on the end. Ask "Do we have more *red* blocks or more *wooden* blocks?" If the child answers "red," ask "Why? Aren't the yellow blocks made of wood, too?" Then, "Do we have more red blocks or more wooden blocks?"

2. Present the strip of paper with the twenty squares drawn on it. Say "These squares are

pictures of our blocks. Draw a line around all the red ones. Now draw a line around all the wooden ones." If the child draws a line around only the yellow ones, ask "But aren't the red ones made of wood, too?"

Discussion

Children up to around seven or eight years of age usually have considerable difficulty understanding that the total class is wider than a large one included in it. The child cannot think simultaneously of the whole and the parts. He forgets the one when he thinks of the other. He has not become able to reverse processes mentally—that is, to think from the parts to the whole and then back to the parts again.

TEST V. ADDITIVE RELATIONS OF PARTS TO WHOLE

The purpose of this test is to determine whether the child can understand that the whole remains constant irrespective of the arrangement of its parts.

Materials Needed

A bag of jelly beans
A bag of M & M's
(Or use two different colors of a breakfast cereal, such as Trix, and change the wording in the directions.)

Directions

1. Place eight jelly beans, in two groups of four, in front of the child and say, "We are going to pretend that these jelly beans are for your snacks today—four for the morning snack and four for the afternoon snack."

   Now place eight M & M's, in two groups of four, on the table and say, "Then we'll pretend that these M & M's are for your snacks tomorrow."

"But, tomorrow you will be so hungry in the morning that you will need to eat this many." (Move three from the afternoon group to the morning group, making groups of 7 and 1.)

2. Ask "Is there the same amount to eat on both days, here (jelly beans) and here (M & M's)?" If the child says no, ask, "But aren't here and here (point to the 4 + 4) the same as here and here (point to the 7 + 1)?"

3. Only if the child does *not* recognize equivalence, ask, "Can we make them (7 + 1) into 4 and 4 again? How? Show me."

4. If the child performs correctly ask "Now are here and here the same?"

"And now?" (changing them back to 7 and 1).

Discussion

As we noted in the first paragraphs, children who do not conceive of number as a constant totality, unchanged through various groupings of its parts, will not profit adequately from instruction in addition and subtraction. They may learn number facts by rote, but that learning will not be useful. The children will not be able to use it to solve problems.

5. Place eighteen M & M's in one group in front of the child. Say, "Divide them so that you and I have exactly the same amount." Then, "Have we both got the same? No? Who has more? Make them so we both have the same."

6. Make two groups of M & M's so there are eight in one group and fourteen in the other. Ask "Where are there more?"

Say, "Make them the same."

After the child moves them ask, "Are they the same now? Show me why."

Discussion

Correct performance of this act requires that the child make the implicit assumption that there is an invariate whole consisting of the elements of the two groups. He must see that whatever change he makes in one group also changes the other group.

TEST VI. CONSERVATION OF LENGTH

Early in the primary grades we begin asking children to measure and to use number lines. If they are to be successful in these activities, they must have reached a level of ability to conserve length. Measurement requires that an object (such as a ruler or a piece of string) remain the same length regardless of changes in its position. The purpose of these four subtests is to determine whether the child has reached the required ability to conserve length.

Materials Needed

Two straight sticks or crayons, of the same length (about 3 to 5 inches)

A piece of clay rolled out into a "rope," 2 inches longer than the sticks

Two strips of paper 12 inches long and ½ inch wide

Scissors

Directions

1. Lay the two sticks side by side, about one inch apart, with their ends aligned exactly:

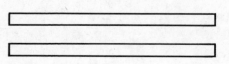

Ask "Are the two sticks the same length, or is one longer than the other?" If the child sees they are the same length, proceed to Step 2.
2. Remove one stick and replace it with the clay rope. Be sure the ends are aligned exactly.

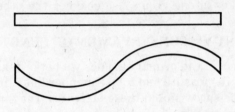

"Are they the same length or is one longer than the other?" If the child says they are different, press him to say why. If he says they are the same, have him run his finger along each in turn. Ask "If there were two little men who had to walk on these, would they have to walk the same distance or would one have to walk farther?"

Discussion

Piaget found that at age 4½ only about 15 percent could answer correctly. At 5½ about 90 percent could answer correctly.

BIBLIOGRAPHY

Articles

Elkind, D., "Piaget's Conservation Problems," *Child Development* 38:15-27, 1967.

———, "Early Childhood Education: A Piagetian Perspective," *The National Elementary Principal* 51:48-55, 1971.

———, "Egocentrism in Young Children," *AAUW Journal* 65:4-6, 1971.

———, "Too Much Matter Over Mind?" *Early Years* December, 1971, pp. 22ff.

Elkind, D., Van Doorninck, W., and Schwarz, C., "Perceptual Activity and Concept Attainment," *Child Development* 38:1153-61, 1967.

Goodnow, J., and Bethon, G., "Piaget's Tasks: The Effects of Schooling and Intelligence," *Child Development* 37:573-82, 1966.

Jennings, F., "Jean Piaget: Notes on Learning," *Saturday Review* May 20, 1967, p. 82.

Piaget, J., "How Children Form Mathematical Concepts," *Scientific American* 189 (20):74-79, 1953.

———, "The Development of Time Concepts in the Child," in P. Hoch and J. Fubin, *Psychopathology of Childhood* (New York: Grune and Stratton, 1955), pp. 34-44.

———, "The Definition of States of Development," in J. Tanner and B. Inhelder, *Discussions on Child Development* (New York: International University Press, 1960), pp. 116-135.

———, "Equilibration and the Development of Structures," in J. Tanner and B. Inhelder, *Discussions on Child Development* (New York: International University Press, 1960), pp. 98-115.

———, "The Child and Modern Physics," *Scientific American* 196 (3):46-57, 1957.

Stendler, C. "Aspects of Piaget's Theory That Have Implications for Teacher Education," *The Journal of Teacher Education* 16:329-35, 1965.

Books

Bearly, M., and Hitchfield, E., *A Guide to Reading Piaget, 1968* (New York: Schocken, 1968).

Elkind, D., *Children and Adolescents: Interpretive Essays on Jean Piaget* (New York: Oxford University Press, 1974).

Flavell, J. *The Developmental Psychology of Jean Piaget* (New York: Van Nostrand Rheinhold, 1963).

Furth, H. *Piaget and Knowledge* (Englewood Cliffs, N.J.: Prentice-Hall, 1969).

Ginsburg, H. and Opper, S., *Piaget's Theory of Intellectual Development: An Introduction* (Englewood Cliffs, N.J.: Prentice-Hall, 1969).

Inhelder, B. and Piaget, J., *The Growth of Logical Thinking from Childhood to Adolescence.* (New York: Basic Books, 1958).

———, *The Early Growth of Logic in the Child* (New York: Harper and Row, 1964).

Maier, H., *Three Theories of Child Development* (New York: Harper and Row, 1965). pp. 75-143.

Phillips, J. *The Origins of Intellect: Piaget's Theory* (San Francisco: W. H. Freeman, 1969).

Piaget, J. *The Child's Conception of Physical Causality* (London: Routledge & Kegan Paul, 1930). (Reprinted in 1965 by Littlefield, Adams & Company, Totowa, N.J.)

———, *The Psychology of Intelligence* (London: Routledge & Kegan Paul, 1950). (Reprinted in 1968 by Littlefield, Adams & Co., Totowa, N.J.)

———, *The Child's Conception of the World* (London: Routledge & Kegan Paul, 1951). (Reprinted in 1969 by Littlefield, Adams & Co., Totowa, N.J.)

———, *Judgment and Reasoning in the Child* (London: Routledge & Kegan Paul, 1951). (Reprinted in 1968 by Littlefield, Adams & Co., Totowa, N.J.)

———, *Play, Dreams and Imitation in Childhood* (New York: Norton, 1951, 1962).

———, *The Child's Conception of Number* New York: Humanities Press, 1952.

———, *The Child's Conception of Time* (New York: Basic Books, 1970).

———, *The Language and Thought of the Child* (London: Routledge & Kegan Paul, 1952). (Reprinted in 1962 by Humanities Press, N.Y.)

———, *The Construction of Reality in the Child* (New York: Basic Books, 1954). (Reprinted in 1971 by Ballantine Books, N.Y.)